Hex codes, or hexadecimal codes, are a way to represent colors in digital devices and web design. Each hex code refers to a very specific color. A hex color is expressed as a six-digit combination of numbers and letters, preceded by a pound sign or hashtag, defined by its mix of red, green, and blue (RGB). The first two letters or numbers refer to red, the next two refer to green, and the last two refer to blue.

The color values are defined as values between 00 and FF. Hex codes are a universal way to describe colors. This book is specifically about shades of yellow.

A is for aesthetic yellow

A

#EFD033

a is for aureolin

a

#FDEE00

C is for cadmium yellow

#FFF600

c is for candle light

c

#FCD917

D is for dodie yellow

#FEDC5D

E is for egg yolk

#FEE33E

e is for energy

#F5D752

F is for festival

F

#FBE96C

f is for fizz

f

#F5CC23

G is for gargoyle gas

#FFDF46

g is for gorse

#FFF14F

H is for hansa yellow

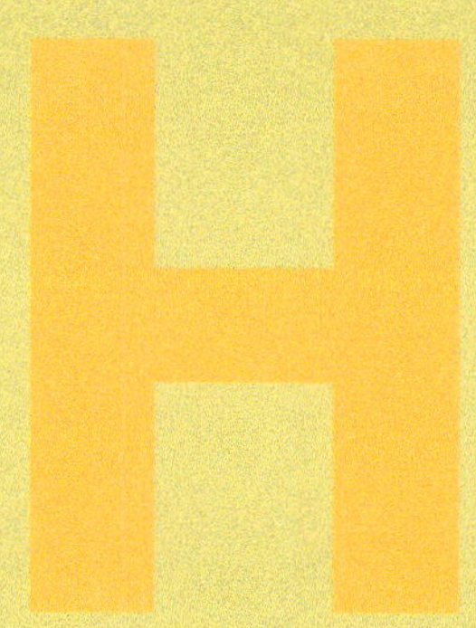

#E9D66B

h is for honey

h

#FFC30B

I is for icterine

I

#FCF75E

i is for indian yellow

i

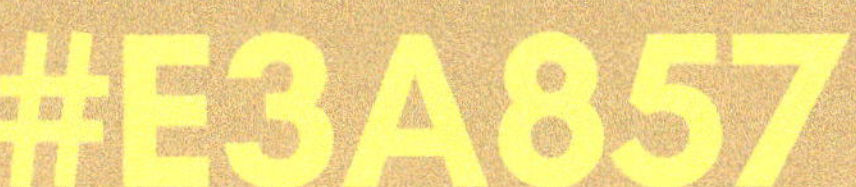

J is for jewelled yellow

J

#9A883E

j is for jonquil

#D7A22A

L is for laguna

L

#F8E463

l is for lemon glacier

#FDFF00

N is for naples yellow

N

#FADA5E

n is for neon gold

n

#CFAA01

O is for oopsy daisy

#FFD67B

o is for orpiment

#EEBD34

P is for paris daisy

P

#FFF46E

p is for portico

#F9E663

Q is for queenly laugh

#FAEDB1

q is for quince apple

q

#EED67D

r is for rubber duck

yellow

#FBE108

S is for sandstorm

S

#ECD540

s is for shooting star

S

#FDE336

T is for titanium yellow

T

#EEE600

t is for tuscany

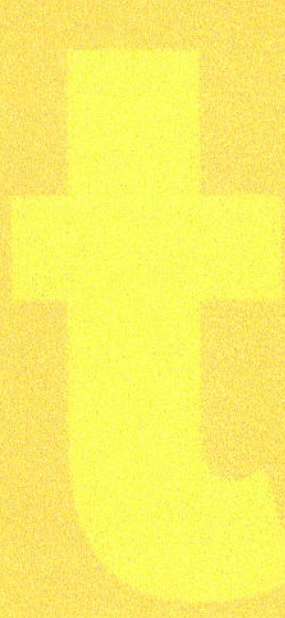

#FCD12A

U is for unmellow yellow

U

#FFFF66

u is for urban yellow

U

#FCCD0D

V is for vis vis

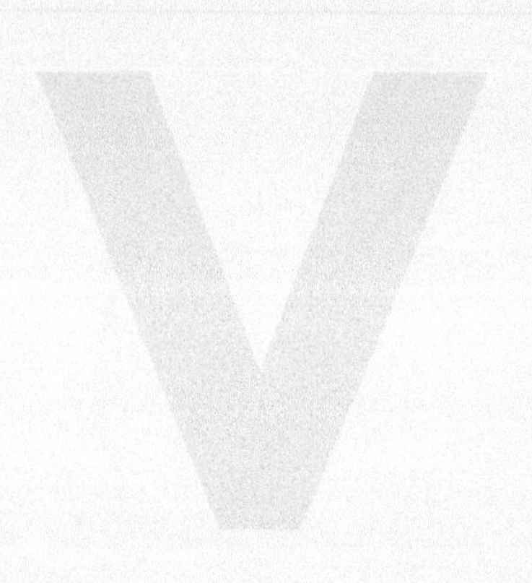

#FFEFA1

v is for vivid yellow

#FFE302

X is for xanthic dark

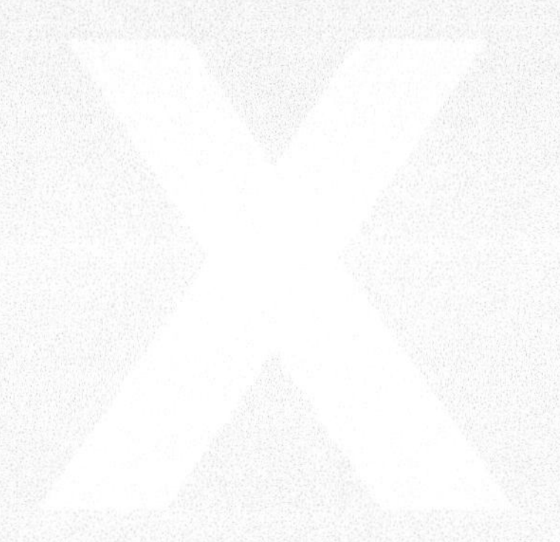

#E6E600

x is for xanthous light

#FFFE00

Y is for yellow tan

#FFE36E

y is for yellow sunshine

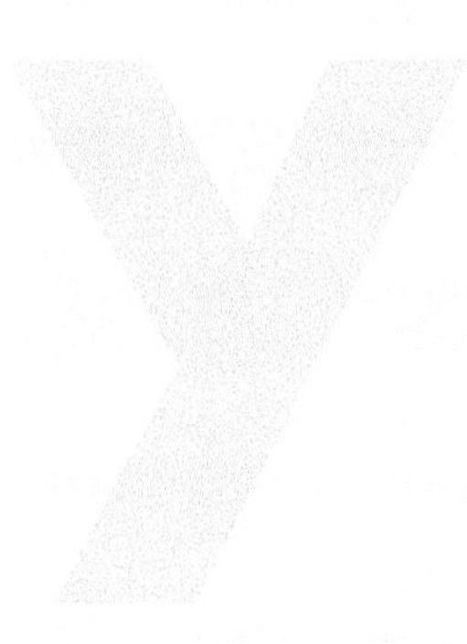

#FFF700

Z is for zany lime

#E8D849

z is for zesty custard

z

#FFEA8E